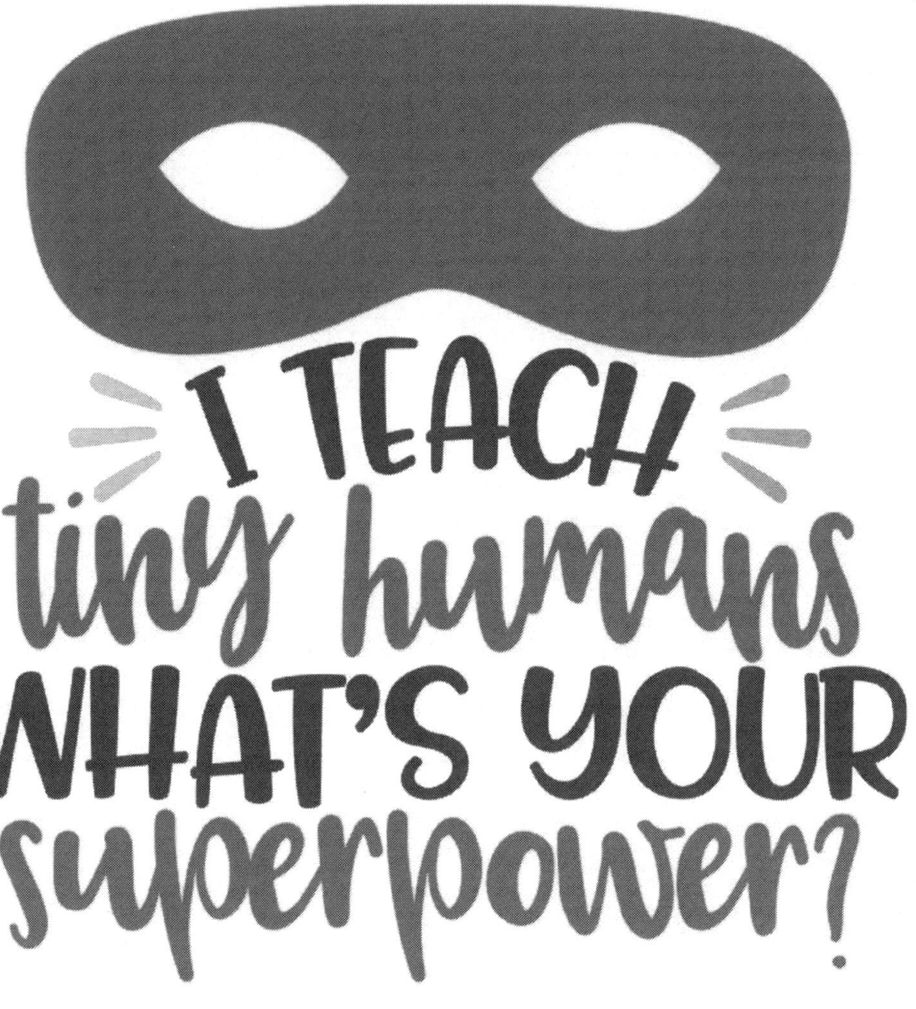
I TEACH
tiny humans
WHAT'S YOUR
superpower?